Mind & Miracles

Poetic Narratives from Thought to Transcendence

Jiya Nadkarni

Dedication

To the divine, whose infinite wisdom serves as my guiding compass, steering me through the shadows and illuminating my path toward the light—my deepest gratitude for your unwavering presence in my life.

To the ephemeral strangers whose brief encounters have graced my journey, thank you for the silent miracles you've bestowed upon me. Each interaction, though transient, has left an indelible imprint on my heart, underscoring the profound interconnectedness we share as human beings in this vast tapestry of existence.

Your presence echoes the beauty of life, reminding me that every moment holds significance and connection.

Preface

The mind is the artisan of our inner world—sculpting reality from thought, coloring the mundane with the hues of imagination, and weaving the fabric of our deepest truths.

*In **Mind & Miracles**, each poem is a testament to that creative power, bridging reason with enchantment, logic with serendipity, and the deliberate with the divine. Here, you will wander through tender hopes and the scars that shape us, traverse the shadows before the dawn of acceptance, and seek the quiet miracles that illuminate our purpose. These verses offer not only reflection but invitation: to pause, listen, and recognize the extraordinary lurking within the ordinary.*

May this collection be your companion on the path of wonder—encouraging you to trust the subtle twist of fate, to honor each heartbeat as a chance for revelation, and to embrace the miraculous in every breath.

Acknowledgements

To those who offer truth with kindness, steady hands in uncertain moments, and quiet presence when it matters most—this work is shaped by you.
Your courage, compassion, and grace live between these lines.

To the strangers whose words, glances, or silent company brought unexpected light—your presence mattered more than you know.
May these pages reflect the quiet strength that surrounds us, seen and unseen.

And to every reader—may something here meet you gently, and remind you to notice the everyday miracles we so often overlook!

Contents

11: Reflections of Truth

- Hush of Time
- Opium of Time
- Resume of Rejection
- Glitch in the Grand Algorithm
- The Infinite Loop

12: The Giving Heart

- Coin Toss
- The Empathy Hotline
- Cubicle Light
- The Quiet Work
- Divine Exchange
- Kindness : The Sneaky Ninja
- Detachment
- Sidewalk Cracks

Mind Ignition

Growing Up

Overwhelmingly, you pour your heart out to the ones
you love,
Knowing how it's always been, Mostly over, than above.
Yet you continue to take the ache,
Our people are bigger than the mistakes they make.
Strong heads have weaker hearts,
Old school, from the very start.

Endless hope eventually turns into a hopeless romance.
Why can't we equally value the essence of bromance?

But whispers of doubt can drown out the voice,
Finding clarity amid the chaos is a choice.
In shadows, we seek the spark that ignites,
A journey of healing through the long, sleepless nights.
For every scar tells a story, a testament to grace,
And love, in its rawness, finds its rightful place.

So let's lift each other, cast aside the fear,
In the dance of connection, let's hold on near.

Loyalty amazes me to a level that I can't handle well.
Rock bottoms are normal and needed—for that's where
our time dwells.

The concept of love excites the blood and muscles;
Soul talk, warm hugs, and smiles can be quite a struggle.

Sugar-coated behaviors and humanity on the edge,
I'd ask you to hold on to love—you might need to
dredge.

Ghosts of the Past

Ghosts of the past, I seek your sage appeal:
Can the world truly find a hope that's real?
Have you noticed how our lives revolve around love,
Or the emptiness that sometimes feels like a shove?
We sway between letting go and holding tight,
Always remember: two wrongs won't make things right.
Words may falter, and pleasures can deceive,
But our purpose in life comes from love we believe.
Create it, feel it, share it, let it glow.

This moment is all we have—let's make our spirits grow.

Fierce

It's common to read in the pursuit of knowledge,
To feed the desire to know where it all leads.
Pushing boundaries can leave us feeling sore;
To even the score, we must confront what we tore.

Ask yourself now—will this all fade away?
Are these hours and hopes just a way to cope?
The way you perceive this world exceeds what we
deserve,
Yet shadows dance where light holds back,
Illuminating the past and embedding our pain.

Stars shine only in the night,
They endure in the daylight too.

The Heart's Permission

Journey of Acceptance

~Anger and Awakening~

In moments of rage, we fiercely unlock,
Frustration at life's relentless tick-tock.
For neglecting ourselves as the chaos unfurled,
Awakening hearts to the truths of this world.

~Chasing the Ace~

In a realm of faces, both nameless and vast,
We yearn for the victories that slip from our grasp.
Instead of pausing, seeking wisdom to find,
We plunge into chaos, leaving wisdom behind.

~Thoughts and Voices~

Our thoughts hold a power much greater than fate;
Our voices, they matter; they're never too late.
Like flowers that bloom with the sun's warm embrace,
With kindness and care, our true selves take place.

~Finding Belonging~

Why wander afar when there's beauty so near?
In the hush of your room, your own truth will appear.
The world is a canvas, your place is your art;
Create from within, let your passions impart.
Share smiles like sunshine—each one is a gift,
For you never know whose spirit it might lift.
No matter the crowd or the stage you may tread,
It's a joy to be you, let your heart be your thread.

~Embracing the Light~

When shadows encircle and doubts start to cling,
Nurture the light, let your spirit take wing.
In the stillness of night or the rush of the day,
Acceptance unlocks every solitary way.
Embrace every flaw, each crack, and each scar;
They guide us through darkness, like beacons, they are.
In loving the journey, the intricate weave,
We discover our strength and the comfort to believe.

Sanctuary of Compassion

Grace

In shadows deep, where sorrow finds its home,
Your heart is in struggle, yet never alone.
You rise and fight through darkness and despair,
Seeking light's embrace, your soul laid bare.

Each day is a battle, a step toward the light,
With quiet strength, a beacon in the night.
With every effort, you reclaim your space,
In this hard-won struggle, you find your bit of grace.

Through tears that fall like rain, healing begins,
A testament to the strength that lies within.

In every moment, you are a true fighter,
And in that power, your spirit shines brighter!

Uniqueness

I tell myself this truth: I embrace life's journey.
In every place, from golden to brown,
There's treasure waiting to be discovered.

I choose to step forward before you leave;
With fewer tears, since you understand this journey of
self-discovery.
It's simply a wish to stand out, to shine brightly.

Come, let's follow the river to the sea;
Let's nurture a forest where dreams may rest.

You'll find me there, beneath it all,
Calmly observing the power of nature in peace.

Together, we'll ignite our spirits and create a legacy of
hope,
Forever connected, celebrating the brilliance of who we
are!

The Sacred Pause

Divine

In case you're wondering where to find me,
Look around, I'm in that in-between,
The space where the sky meets the sea,
The whispers of trees, And the edges of your dreams.
Close enough, almost to touch,
But slightly out of reach!
I'll be on the moon and among the stars— But never
really far.

And I'm always there, Inside your heart!

Something

The realm to be, the realm to see.
When you're neither awake nor asleep,
It's a place where your creativity blossoms,
A space where you might not even recognize yourself.

In this quiet grove, you still love the trees,
Their earthy pine scent filling every breath.
Sunlight drapes your bare skin like a gentle caress.
Close your eyes, and you feel your heartbeat,
Slow and deep,
While the dog on your chest
Forsakes his treat for sleep.

One day, when your mind is calmer,
You may find the ability to read books again.
Some people love you, even if they don't know you.
This doesn't always need to feel like a burden or a
wound.
It can still feel good to write from time to time, even if
you don't share your words with anyone.
Things will not always be this way.

You don't have to believe that, but you need to believe in
something.

The Mind's Playground

I park my thoughts on swing and slide,
And watch them giggle, dart, collide.
No ticket is needed—all are free,
To roam the fields of clarity.

I'm guardian of this merry lot,
Yet laugh when one forgets its spot.
In stillness, chaos takes a bow,
And every thought's a friendly "Howdy, how?"

In this playground of the mind,
I find the joy that's often blind.
With every twist and every turn,
New lessons bloom, and insights churn.

Snack break of the Soul

Pause your scroll, dear restless heart,
Let meditation be your tart.
A nibble here—a breath or two,
Savor calm like honeydew.

No calories, just mental cheer;
Mind-M&Ms melt stress to the bier.

Crunch on stillness, bite into peace,
Repeat until your chaos ceases.

Flight of Courage

Leap of Faith

Faith is that daring circus stunt,
A trapeze swing in mid-air.
You trust the rope, despite the front,
Of butterflies that tangle there.

"Let go!" the inner coach will tease,
While stomach flips like a pastry breeze.
Yet in that flight, you find your wings,
And sometimes even pull off flings.

So, clutch your doubts, then let them drop,
And watch your spirit pirouette nonstop!

Embers of Intention

Not all fire is loud.
Some burn like a whisper,
A quiet decision at dawn,
Before the coffee brews,
Before the world asks who, you are.

Intent, is the spine of action,
The unseen hand that steadies,
When motivation forgets your name.

It does not shout,
It does not seek applause.
It simply stays.

It stays,
When your knees ache,
When your hands tremble,
When no one is watching.

And that staying,
That quiet, sacred staying,
Is where, God leans the closest.

Heart's Odyssey

The heart set sail without a chart,
On seas where wonder meets lost art.
It drifted through love's masked domain,
Whispered secrets to the rain.

Bruised by shadows, stretched by doubt,
Silence cracked, then roared about.
Yet still it pulses, scar and song,
A quiet compass, fierce and strong.

For strength divine, through night's embrace,
Transforms the storm, restores the grace.
And hope, the lantern ever bright,
Guides weary hearts, back to light.

Motorcycle Prayer

Let the wind remind me I am free,
But never far from humility.
Let each mile mark where fear was shed,
And courage took the lead instead.

Grant me eyes sharp on the turn,
And hands that know when not to burn.
A heart at peace beneath this leather,
In sun, In storm, In any weather.

Forgive the haste, the need for flight,
Some of us heal best at speed, not height.
And when I stop, let stillness stay,
Like chains at rest at close of day.

If I must fall, then let it teach,
If I must ride, then let me reach,
Not just for roads that twist and bend,
But for the truths that never end.

Amen to motion, grace and grit,
To sacred roads, and peace in it.

Forged by Trials

Alchemical Wealth

Wealth hums with promise—and peril.

It erects a haven and fuels aspirations ahead.
Yet without intention, it feels quite void,
True affluence flourishes where generosity is employed.
In treasured moments and kindness bestowed,
In endeavors pursued, though accolades are owed.
Harmonize your treasures with your deeper aim,
Let altruism be the essence of your claim.

Each coin expended becomes a testament true,
A manifestation of faith in the bonds we construe.

Divine Typos

Every "sorry" you misspell, every apology you stumble,
Is God's editorial comment in the margin:

"Meaning here—yes, but craft it with grace."

Mistakes are the red ink of the cosmos,
Pointing out the words that matter most.

So let your failures bloom like typographical miracles,
They're proof that the Editor in Chief still cares!

Fear's Gentle Transformation

I captured fear in attire quite chic,
Served it brew—transformed its mystique.
"Come, join me," I beckoned with a playful smirk,
"Let's stir up some whimsy, let mischief work!"

In a flash, fear turned into a shy friend,
Patting my chest as it sipped in the blend.

Exhilaration blooms when rivals break bread,
Timid hearts find their courage, and old doubts are shed.

Guilty Pleasure

The purest pleasures that guilt can bring
Are like the tickling around a wound or sting.
The tickle leaves no sweetness behind,
But the wound heals, leaving a mark of its kind.
Is it a scar or a bittersweet memory
We keep tucked away in our hearts' deep entry?
Too afraid for the world to see,
Not daring to voice what we won't set free.

You sleep over your thoughts each day,
Hoping for healing, in your own way.

Oh, dear child, did you not know,
God has ineffable ways to help you grow,
To wave away despair, and with grace, let go.

Rediscovered Innocence

More to You...

Radiant skin and perfect curves,
A billion views and restless nerves.
A sturdy frame with graceful lines,
Chilled hearts and aimless times.

Our appearances carried a cost, I found.
When did being soul-less become the norm around?
I thought the world thrived on love and strife,
Now, there's no common ground in this life.

Modern culture brings a death of shame,
The body matters more than age or name.

A strong wave of emotion can lead to despair too,
The emptiness that once floated has taken root and
grown.
My love, there's more to me—and more to you.

Balloons

While young, we tied heartstrings to helium dreams,
Hoping they'd carry us to carve names on the moon.

Bruised knees bore battle wounds from monsters we'd
slain ;
Heart howls echoed in the rulers of rain.

Branches became towers to gaze upon realms,
Stormy waves test our grasp on our helms.

Yet even dreamers awake feel shadows at their feet.
We traded books for grown-up wars—balloons gave their
defeat.

"The real world's a war," you said of wild hearts;
Yet joy must always endure in our finite parts.

Combinations

What if the earth wasn't round,
Mistakes were considered profound?

What if the sky lacked its azure hue,
And we could repair our hearts with glue?

What if everyone could be touched
Only when sorrows were discussed?

What if oxygen were granted
Only when we were self-reliant?

What if our fury could be quantified
Not by the losses we've endured?

What if maturity was measured by wisdom
Instead of just the passage of time?

You might be reckless when solitude is near,
And passionate, even when gripped by fear.
You could be warm-hearted, but perhaps lacking charm,
Loving so deeply that it risks causing harm.

You could be curious without knowing your aim,
Yet remain calm through the pressure and strain.
You might be the one they cherish and need,
Only to realize they're seeking a new breed.

You could learn and blossom, vibrant and bold,
But still yearn for a hug, to feel safe and whole.
Confident and daring, standing proud and true,
Yet find yourself irritable, feeling blue.

You could express countless words of sincere love,
But still walk away nursing wounds from above.

You might be noble and wise,
Yet still find yourself in last place—calling it fate that
defies.

In your darkest hour, you could still find grace;
For beyond this, nothing else matters—it has ceased.

Meditation

A silent buzz beneath my skull,
Is that a bee or cosmic lull?
I sit, I float, I crane my ear,
To catch that chuckle crystal-clear.
It's neither a bug nor a haunted ghost,
But me in Zen, at my roast.

With each "Om," I snort in delight,
Tickled pink by inner light.

Echoes of Gratitude

Sacred Mosaic

God shows up as the child's grin in morning traffic,
As a phone call from home just when tears rise,
As a bird tracing patterns in a steel sky.
Love takes shape in every offering,
A meal shared, a hand-held, a word of truth.

The world is rich with wondrous sights;
If we open our hearts and embrace the lights.
In every moment, a beauty sings,
Transforming our lives into joy that springs.

The Stranger Who Knew Me

He said:
"You dropped this,"
And handed me my bus pass.

But he looked at me
Like I mattered.

Not flirtation,
Something gentler.

Like he saw my sadness and nodded
as if to say, "Yes. I know.
Keep going anyway."

And then he was gone.

Sometimes, God wears
Cargo shorts and disappears at the next stop.

Ephemeral Grace

He held the door as I juggled bags and deadlines,
We shared a laugh about gravity and grind.
I never learned his name, and I never will.
Still, the memory haunts me with its simplicity:
How a fragment of connection can rearrange a heart.

That passing echo taught me:

We are always more alive in the company of strangers.

A Thousand Brief Encounters

Every queue at a café, every halt at a crosswalk,
We impact lives in ephemeral encounters:
A nod, a door graciously held,
A shared umbrella between passing strangers.

None of these bonds endure, and none request your
number.
Yet each leaves an imprint on your heart.

Our days are woven with these flickers of connection,
And together they chart a cosmos of belonging.

Inhale the Possible

Air

Tell me, how is it fair,
When our lives are but a gasp for air?

Where stars scarce find a chance to blink,
Ere we collapse on existence's brink?

Why must we race, only to fall apart?
It's time to learn what stirs our hearts,

Before our final trip around the sun,
Before distant Neptune's course is run.

It is a tragedy, truly, that we leave,
With so much more still left to perceive.

Just as we grasp what breath entails,
We are expected to exhale.

Numbers

When I was in second grade,
my teacher would ask,
"How are you today, on a scale of one to ten?"
Ten meant *"I'm great!"*
Anything less sighed, *"Not today, Miss."*
But numbers never sat right with me —
they twisted, rebelled inside my mind.

I thought in colors instead.

January 21st:
Soft silver mist, hovering between thought and dream.

February 13th:
A bruise of blues and violets, tucked into the folds of my blanket.

March 9th:
Pale peach, stretching shyly toward spring.

April 13th:
Charcoal dusk, silent weight pressing against my ribs.

May 7th:

Rose-gold and ivory— the quiet hues of hands that hold without asking, Of love that asks for nothing.

June 8th:

Deep emerald, vibrating with the breath of summer storms.

July 12th:

School-bus yellow, hurtling me toward the wild ache of freedom.

August 17th:

Sun-soaked green, restless, reaching beyond the trees.

September 22nd:

Russet and amber, leaves crumbling under quiet steps.

October 19th:

Maroon and smoke, stitched into cooling air.

November 22nd:

Burnt orange and wine, gratitude steeped in longing.

December 15th:

Midnight blue, flecked with sleeping stars.

Ten years later, I still paint my days in color.
Summer blazes bright green across my ribs,
Winter hums in violets and ocean blues,
Grey lingers at the seams.
And sometimes—
Sometimes I am all white,
Washed in soft gold,
Each second breathing itself into my skin.
And in those rare moments,

I am simply, endlessly—grateful.

Tender Hopes

An unanswered prayer, steadfast in composure and soft apologies.
Look at your butterfly wings,
Torn from your body by a child's curious, innocent hands.
It reminds me of empty envelopes,
Shredded at the edges,
No longer holding promises,
No longer capable of those reckless, frolicking flights.

And so, these quiet deductions spill from me,
How everyone is struggling to be stitched whole again,
How victories slip by unseen,
Because we don't know how to name our losses out loud.
The world's harshness falls heavy on our tender hopes,
Yet somehow, somehow,
They strengthen, gripping tighter onto God's rope.

The Inner Pact

Called by Name

Maybe it's faith, Maybe belief,
That turns a longing into relief.
For when we trust with soul and mind,
The world, in quiet ways, aligns.
What we desire, we shape, we mold;
Not through chance, but hearts made bold.
And when it comes, we call it fate,
Or miracle—just running late.

But truth be told, it's not by chance;
It's born from every inward glance.

Believe in light—Watch light unfold.
Believe in dark—It takes its hold.

The divine arrives when called by name,
And so does sorrow, just the same.
We are woven forms of thought and flame,
No two of us are quite the same.
We walk as mirrors, side by side,
Where all beliefs and truths collide:
The good, the bad, the fierce, the kind,
The cruel, the tender, all entwined.

All here at once, beneath one sky,
Just human spirits passing by.

Layers of Clarity

I'm melted white in layers— that's all you see.
Inside, wine flows— Divine clarity.
My heart crunches and climbs, emotions too deep;
My ego lies dormant; I've outgrown that need.

Speak to the soul— It knows what's good,
For me, for you, for all the hood.
New pages turn like old,

What's written proves we lived,
Yet never the same.

Reflections of Truth

Hush of Time

52

Call it rational thinking or creative reasoning,
Inbred genetics or years of seasoning.

A moment arrives, so the undersigned,
Mindful eyes behold the sublime.
Today, autumn leaves brush my hair,
Wind urging me forward—I step into the air.
A storm of feeling envelops my core,
My faithful dog trembles at the door.

We stand beneath a silent tree line;
No soul in sight—winter's hush defines.
A shiver runs down my spine,
A memory etched in time's design.

Opium of Time

Low tides and towering peaks,
Dawn's tender whispers and dusky twilight streaks,
Solitary nights and murmured truths,
Expansive hearts within diminutive booths.
Golden-coated falsehoods and ephemeral truths,
Affairs of passion and hearthstone hues,
Inherited traits and years of maturation,
Lush conversations, ingrained habituation.
A touch of madness, relentless pursuit,
Indelible moments, cyclical roots,
Radiant grins and hollowed gazes,
Yet through the cracks, hope softly raises.
Inevitable orbits, unseen hands,
Empathy, genesis, actions, and strands,
Velocity and radiance, mercy, and strife,
Humanity's struggle, but light guides our life.

Loving and wounding — the opium of time,
Yet every heartbeat is a chance to climb.

Resume of Rejection

Objective: Uncover the spark that sets my soul ablaze

Experience:
Twenty-seven résumés devoured by digital voids
Three handwritten love notes stamped "Return to Sender"
One half-drafted novel buried beneath college term-paper detritus

Skills:
Rebounding with phoenix-fire resilience
Eyebrow choreography—raising questions, dropping truths

References:
Each "No" that cracked open a new horizon
Every slammed door echoing an uncharted path

Divine Footnote:
God's executive search is whispered
Through a cosmic rejection hotline
And I'm the final callback.

Glitch in the Grand Algorithm   55

I scrolled the cosmos like a newsfeed,
Liked a star, left no comment,
Subscribed to the Comet's newsletter,
Yet here I am, a glitch in the grand algorithm.
Existence is a meme that riffs on itself,
The laugh-track of quantum particles colliding.
And in the infinite scroll, I find:

The punchline was me all along!

The Infinite Loop

You are the echo in the canyon,
A voice that never tires of praising itself.

I tell you once, you whisper it back.
I tell you twice, you become the mountain.
Tell you again—now the sun leans in,
Light rebounding off your every facet.

Beware: At the edge of this loop,
You might just outshine the compliment.

The Giving Heart

Coin Toss

Money rattles like loose change in my pocket,
A promise and a threat in the same copper clink.

I flip a coin: heads, I buy a coffee ;
tails, I give it away.
Either way, generosity wins.

Because wealth survives in the moments we choose to
spend it,
On laughter, on meals shared, on hands held tight.

True currency is the warmth you leave behind,
And that never depreciates.

The Empathy Hotline

I ring your heart with a silent dial,
tuning in for every trial.

No canned script, no corporate guise,
"How can I help?" with earnest eyes.

Kindness needs no neon glow,
it listens close when tempests blow.

Your sorrows to share, my ear to lend,
empathy's hotline: friend to friend.

Cubicle Light

A neon pulse sustains our minds,
While ambition threads through spreadsheet lines.

Folders tower like muted pleas,
yet sparks ignite in shared reprieves.

One whispered "thank you" shifts the weight,
and solved conundrums clear the slate.
Hope takes flight on purpose's wings,

As dawn's glow seeps through filing rings.
Even here, where gray walls close,
Divine light dances in cubicle rows.

The Quiet Work

You don't need a title,
It's how you show up.

You turn the key,
Answer the calls,
Hold the line
When no one's watching.

You keep the room immaculate,
Calm the swirling chaos,
Snuff the smallest spark.

In all that unseen labor,
Purpose drifts like incense:
Subtle, unclaimed,
Yet unmistakable.

Sacred things don't always shine.
Sometimes they endure.

Divine Exchange

You bought the shoes,
Didn't mend your self-worth.

You took the trip,
Still cried in the Airbnb shower.

You hustled hard,
The bank account smiled,
Your soul barely yawned.

Then one day you gave away
The last cookie you craved,
and felt, inexplicably,
Full.

Turns out,
The Return On Investment on kindness
Isn't tracked in spreadsheets,
but damn,
It compounds!

Kindness :
The Sneaky Ninja

Quiet as moonlight, swift as a breeze,
Kindness tip-toes in ninja-knees.

It plants a grin behind your back,
Defuses frowns with a silent knack.

No fanfare needed—just a knowing wink,
A jasmine-scented lift before you blink.

It slips in-jokes like whispered art,
A gentle shove that warms the heart.

By dawn it's gone—no trace to show,
Yet souls still glow with its soft echo.

Detachment

I thought love was a fragile vase,
handle gently, fear the cracks.

But love's more like the helium craze:
it lifts you high and skips the facts.

So I hold my heart with open palms,
let it drift in jubilant qualms.

No cage, no leash, just buoyant grace,
it floats away with a smiling face.

And when it soars into the blue,
I bow and smile, for it was never mine to strew.

Sidewalk Cracks

Golden light pools in city seams,
where dandelions push through concrete.
You almost walk past—too busy to notice,
until the glow halts you in mid-step.

There, life insists on beauty,
even when you've forgotten to look up.

Hope finds you, always, in the smallest cracks.